I0463624

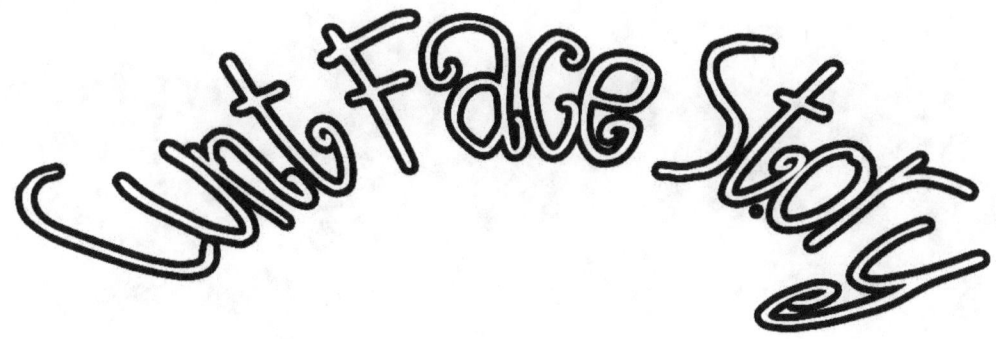

Cunt Face Story

Adorable Swear Word To Color

FOR STRESS RELEASING

By

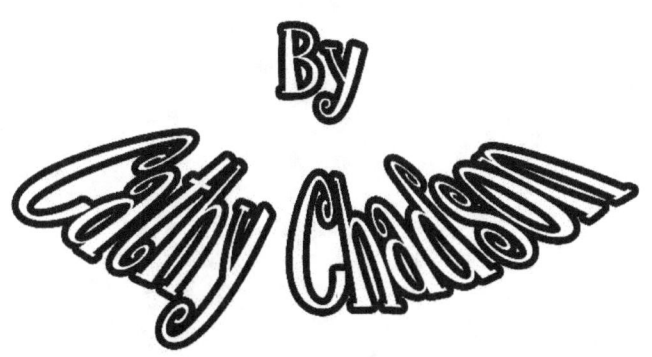

Cathy Chadison

Copyright © 2017 by Cathy Chadson

All rights reserved worldwide. No part of this publication may be reproduced or distributed in any form or by any means, mechanical, electronic or stored in a retrieval or database system, without written permission from the copyright holder.

Happy Coloring

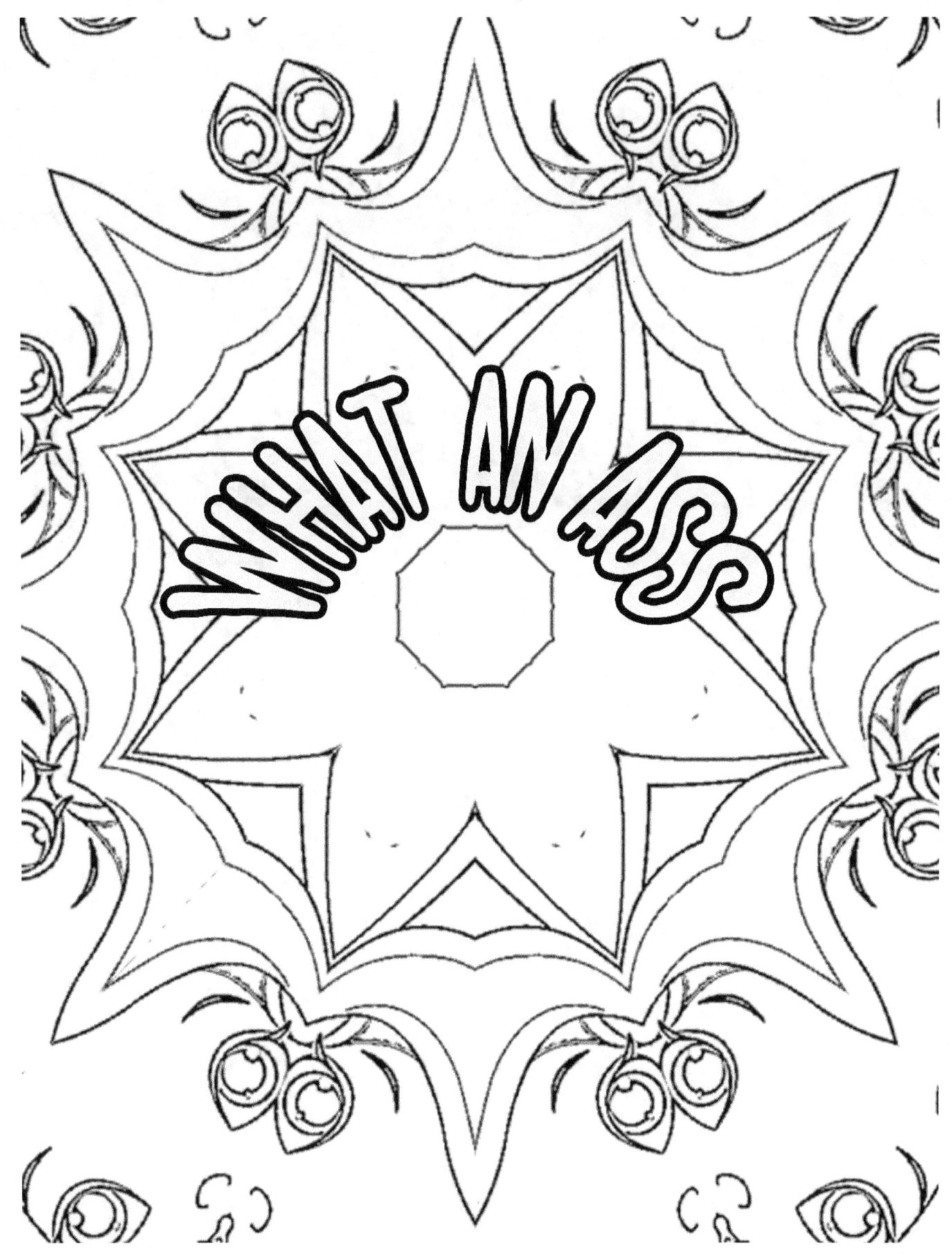

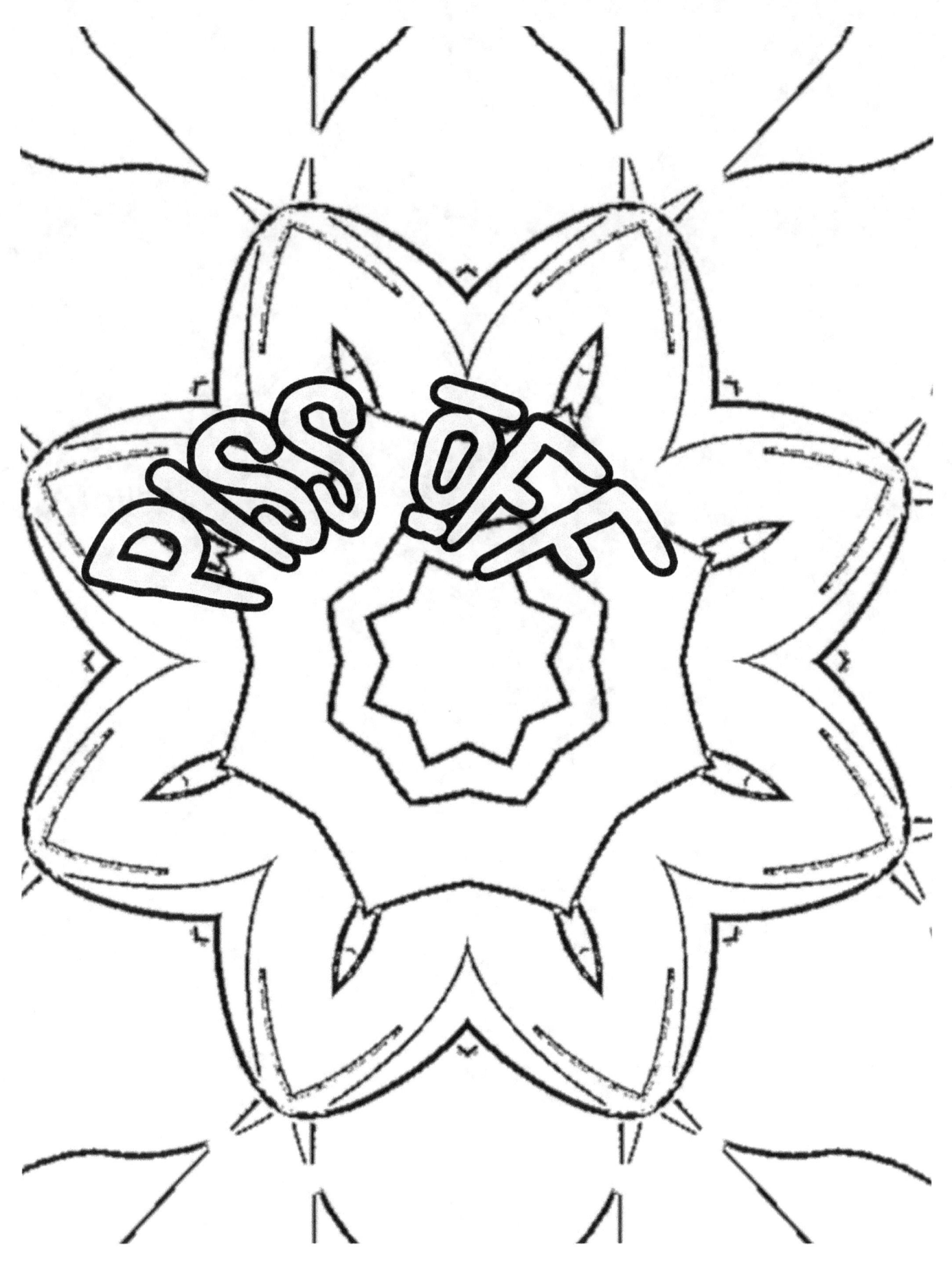

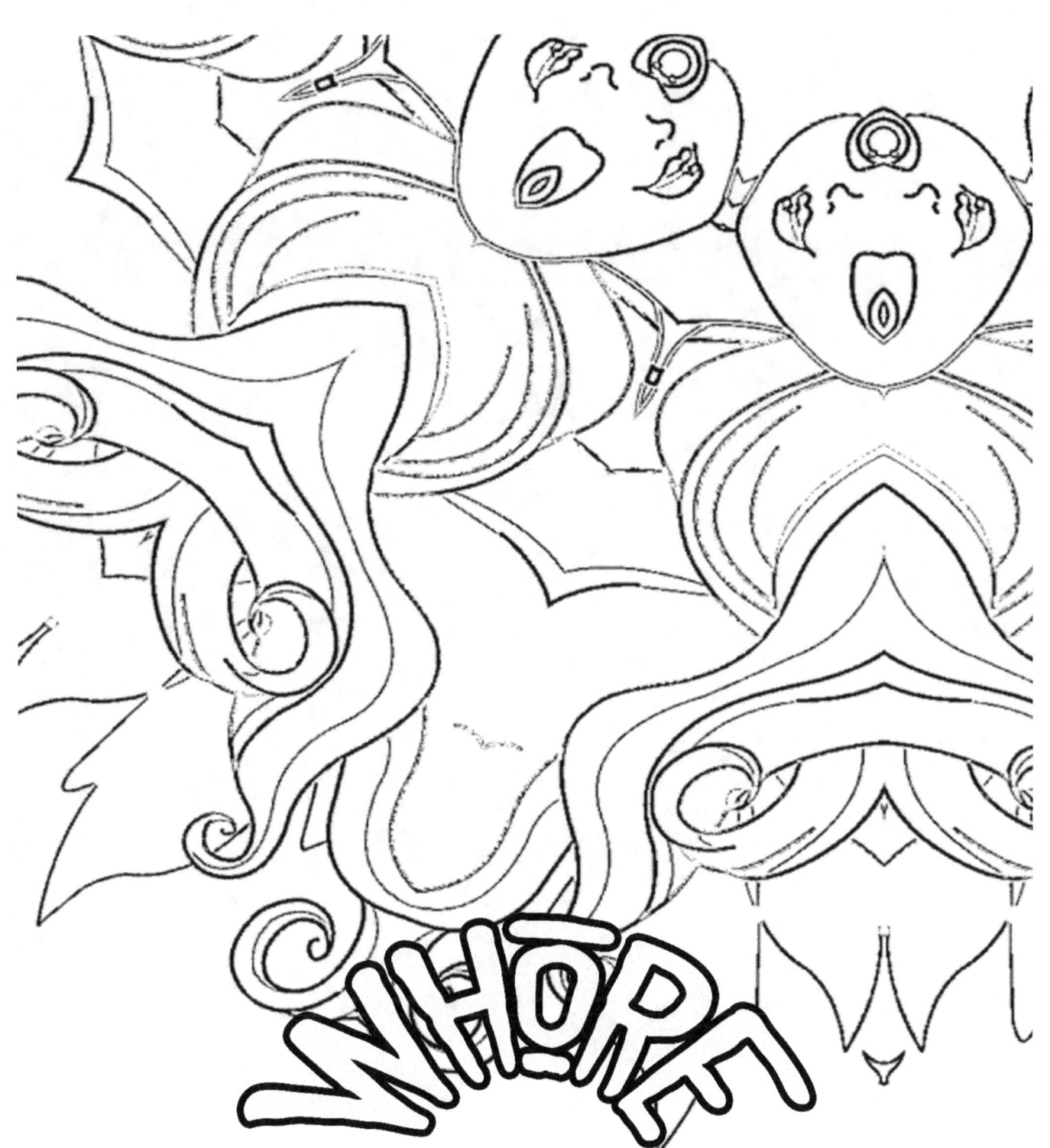

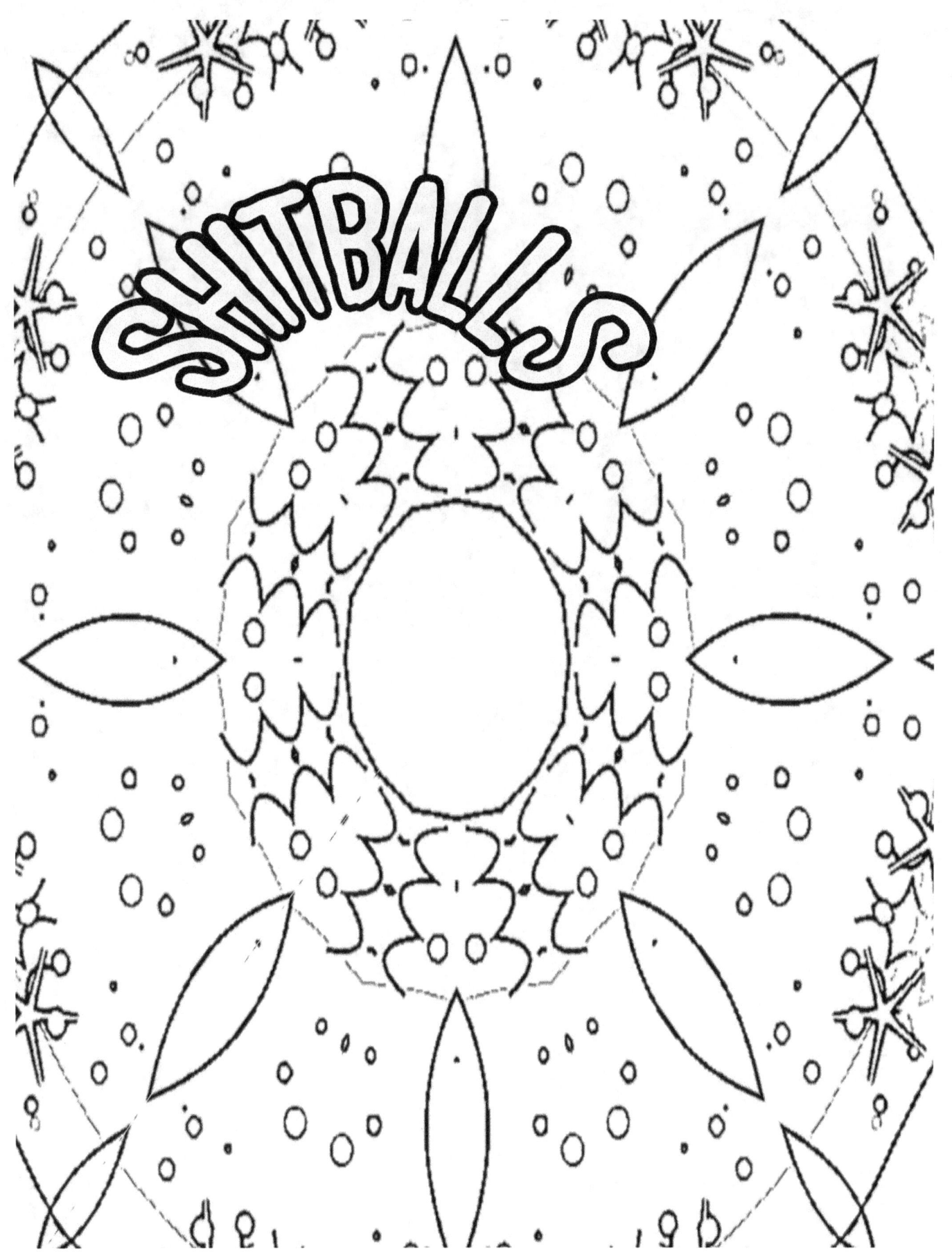

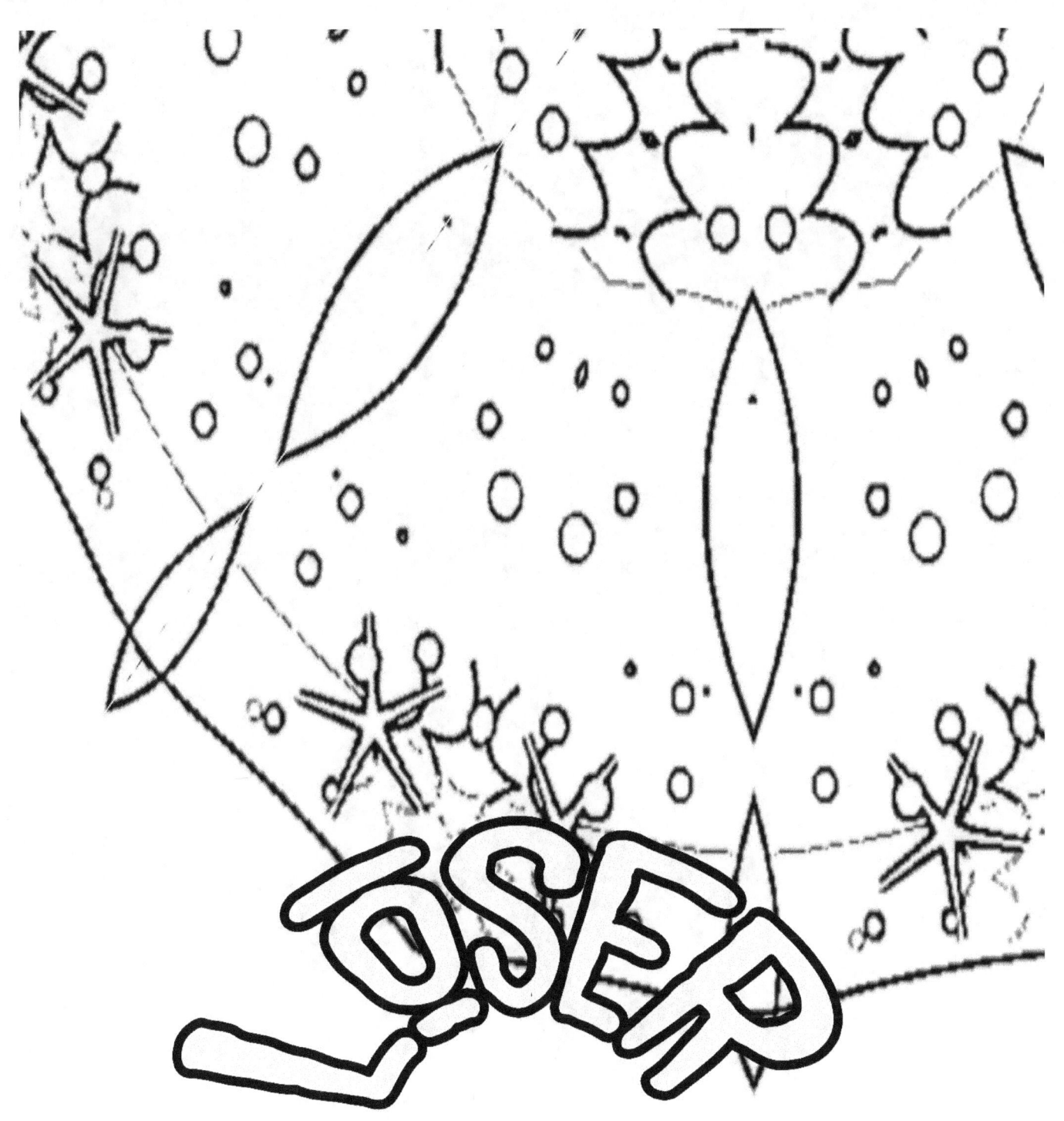

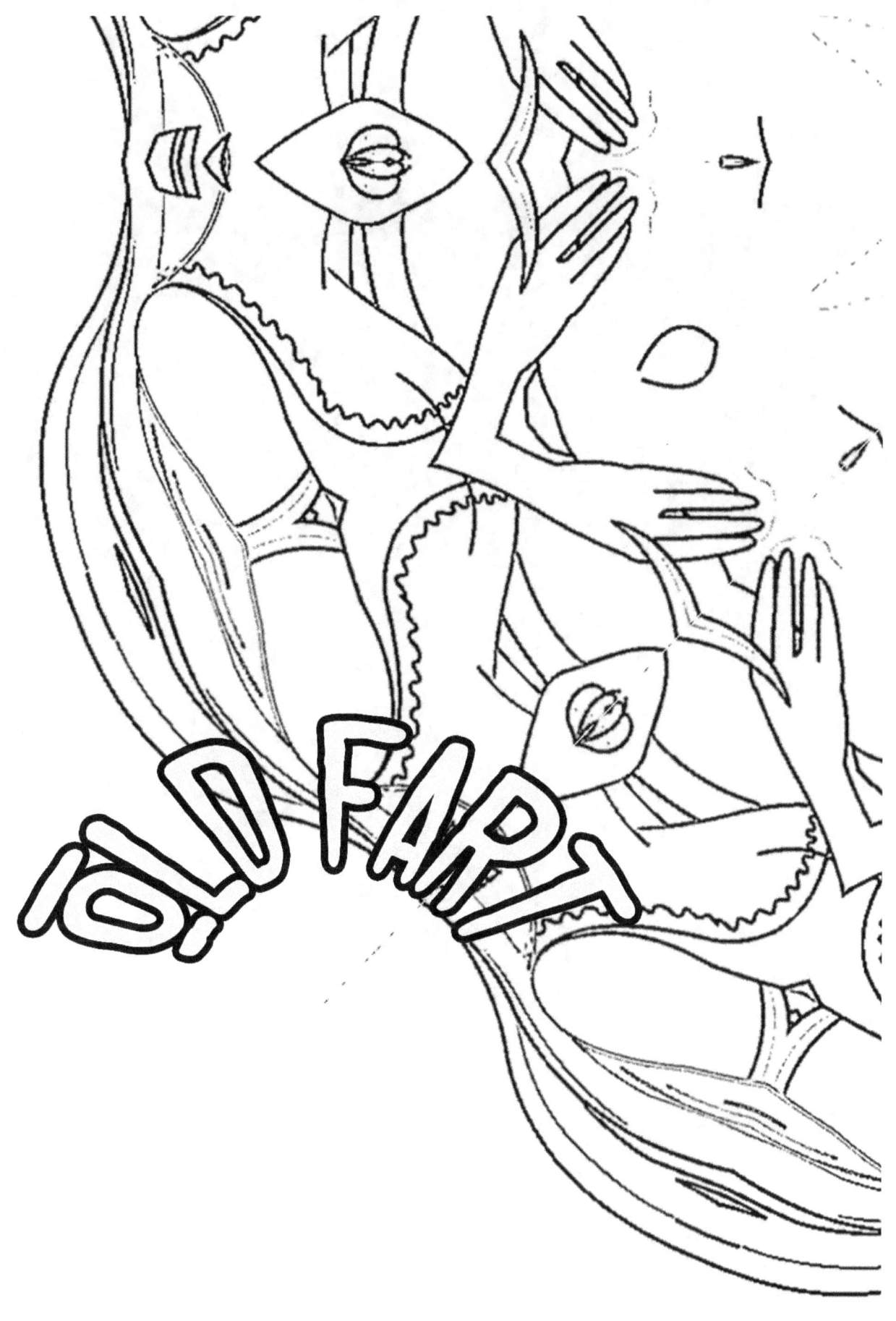

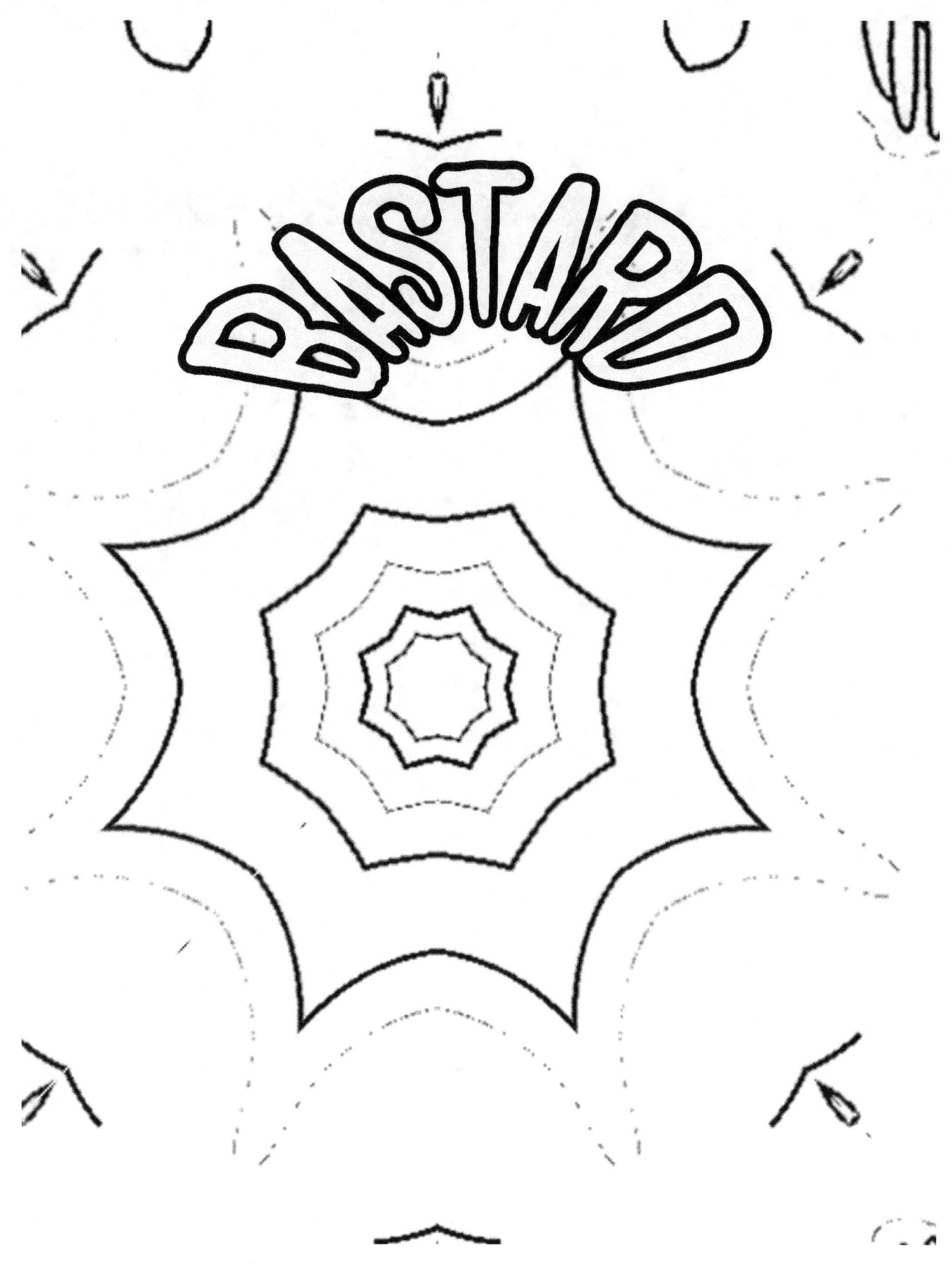

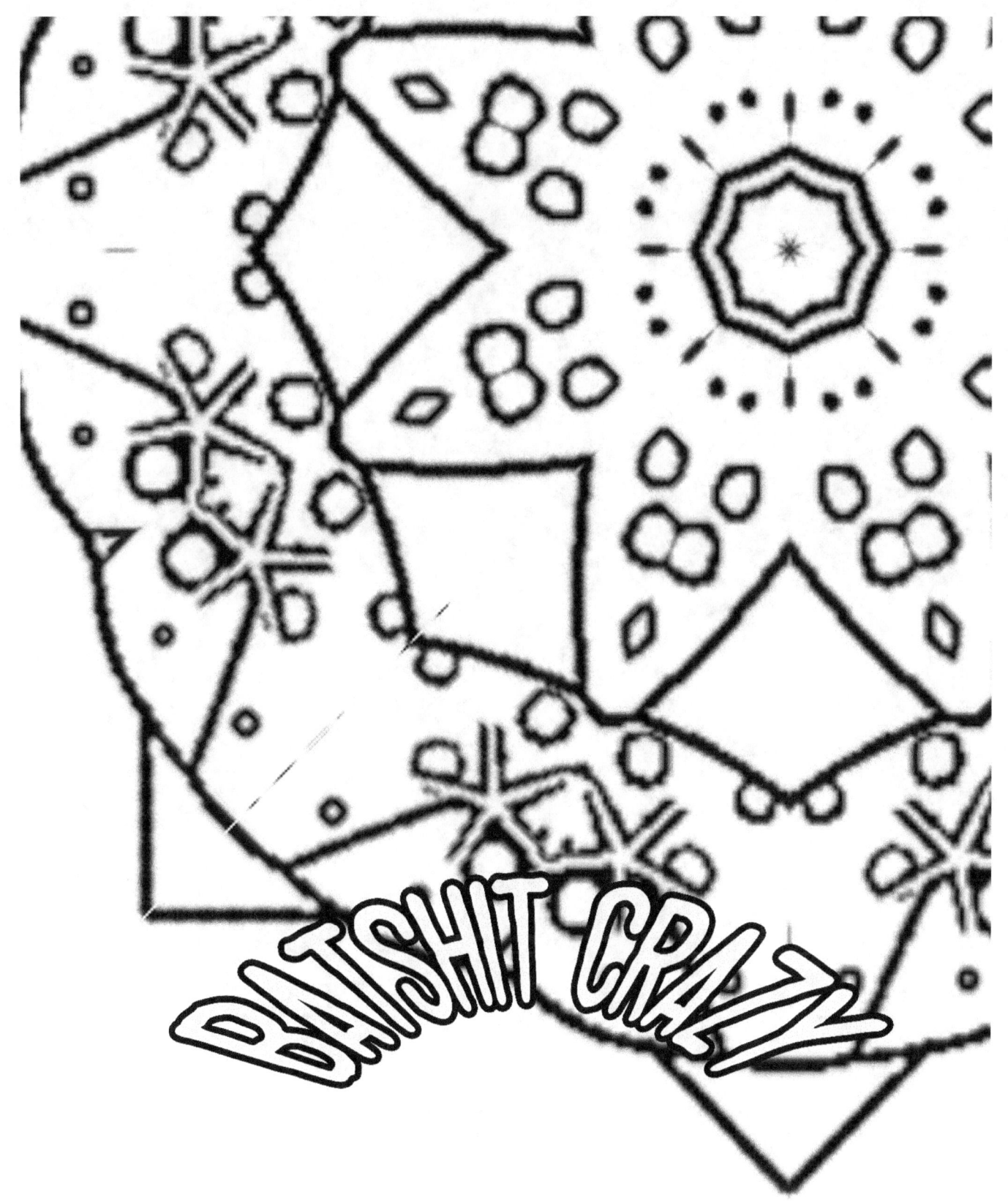

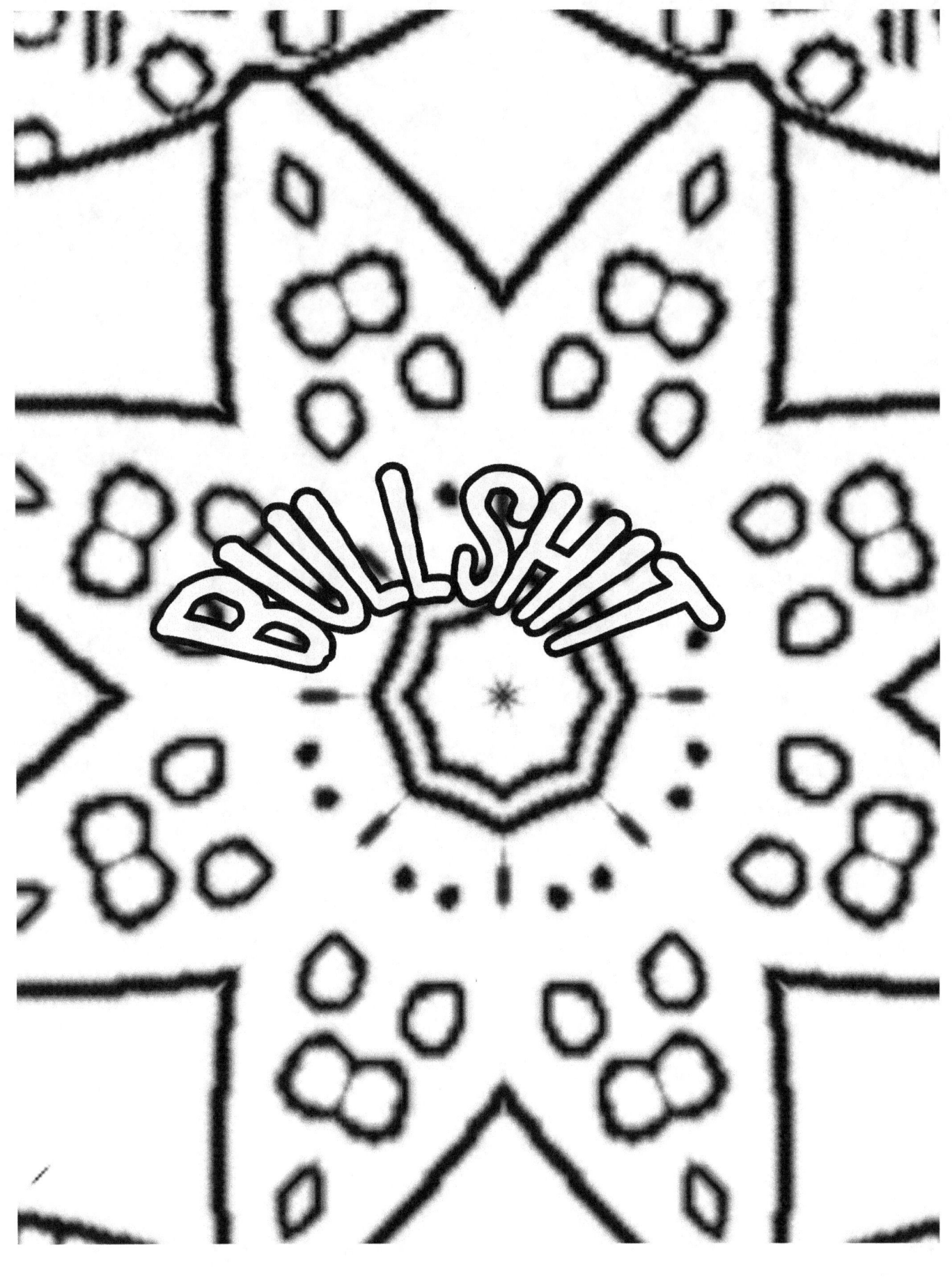

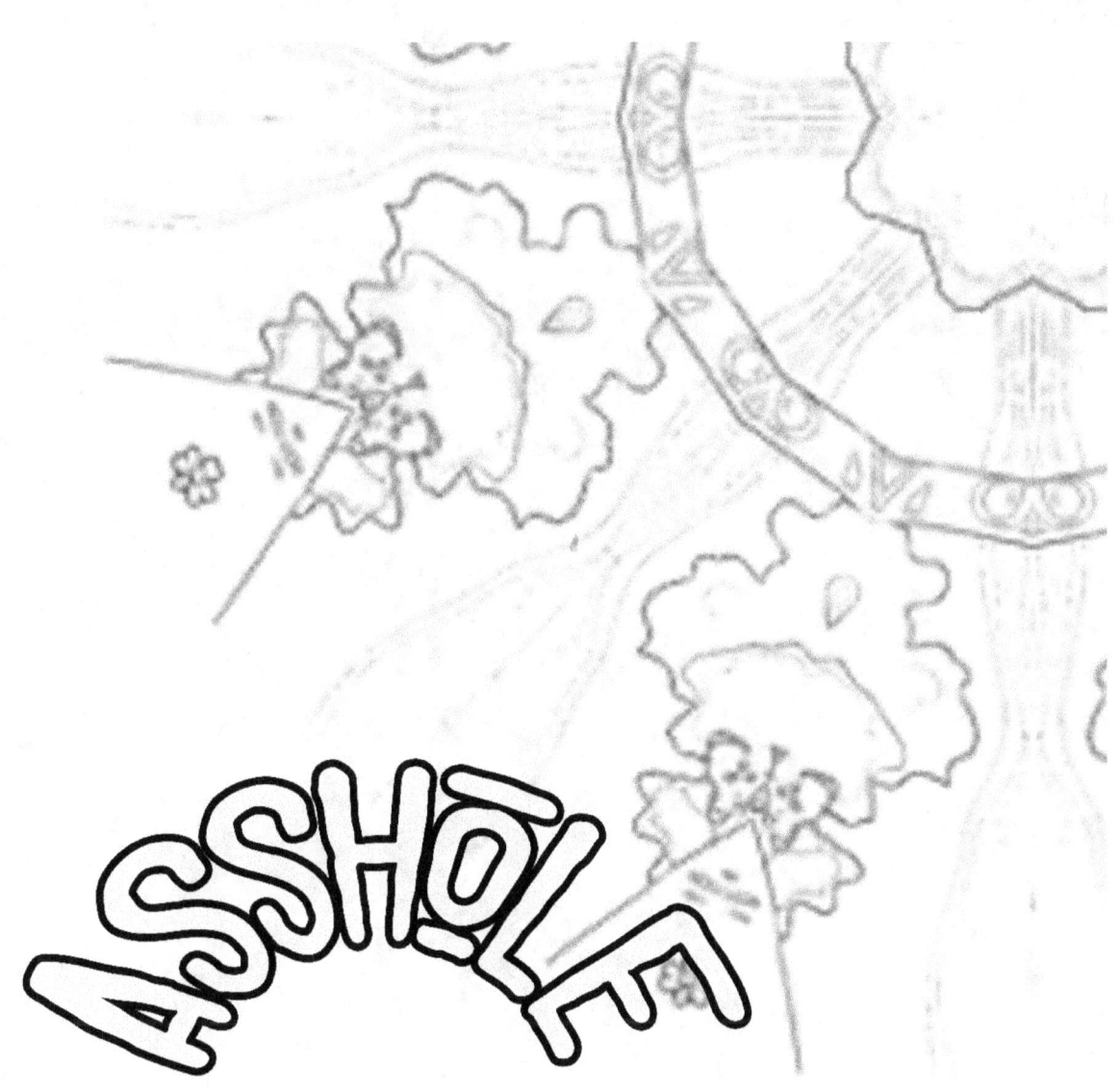

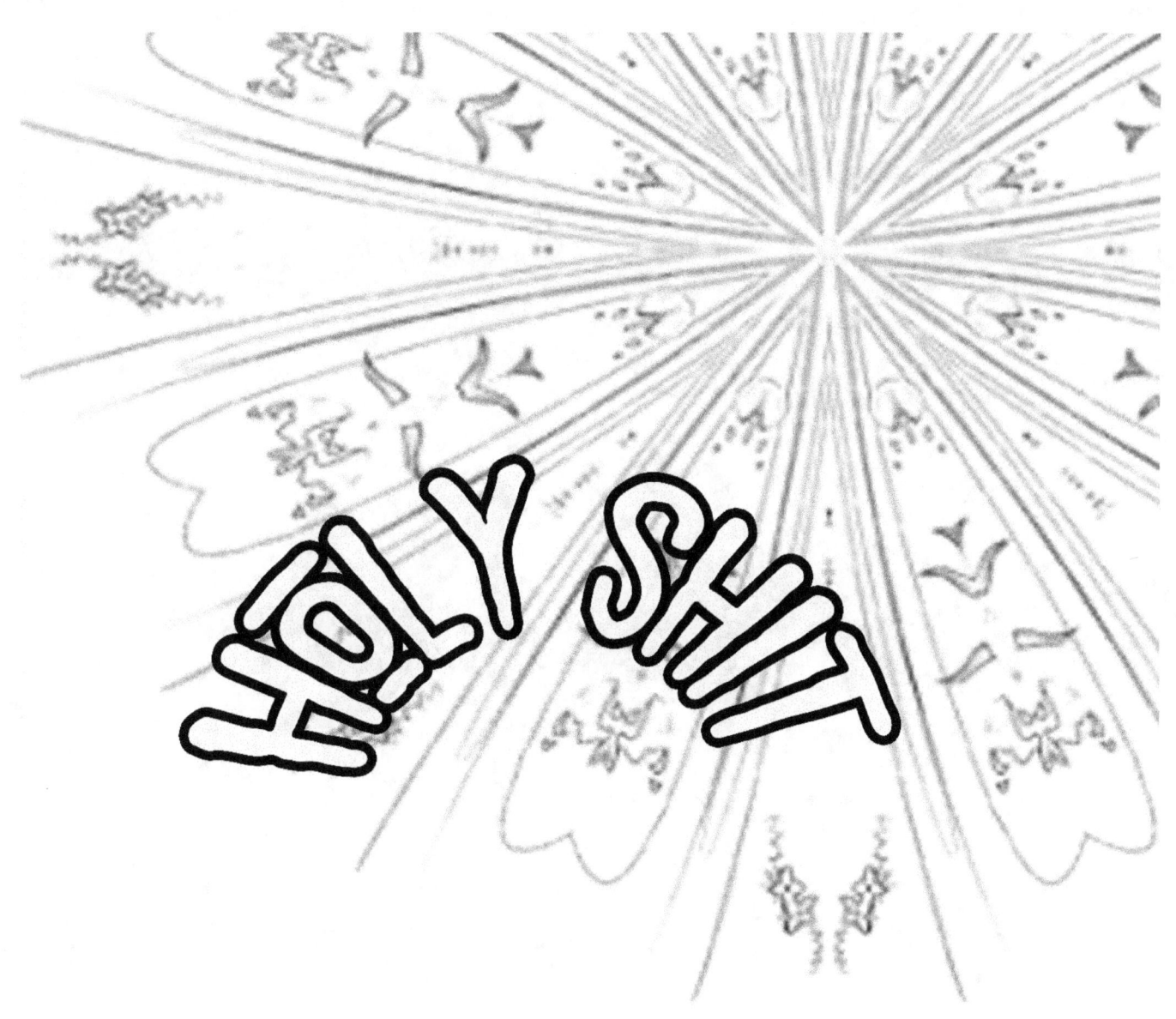

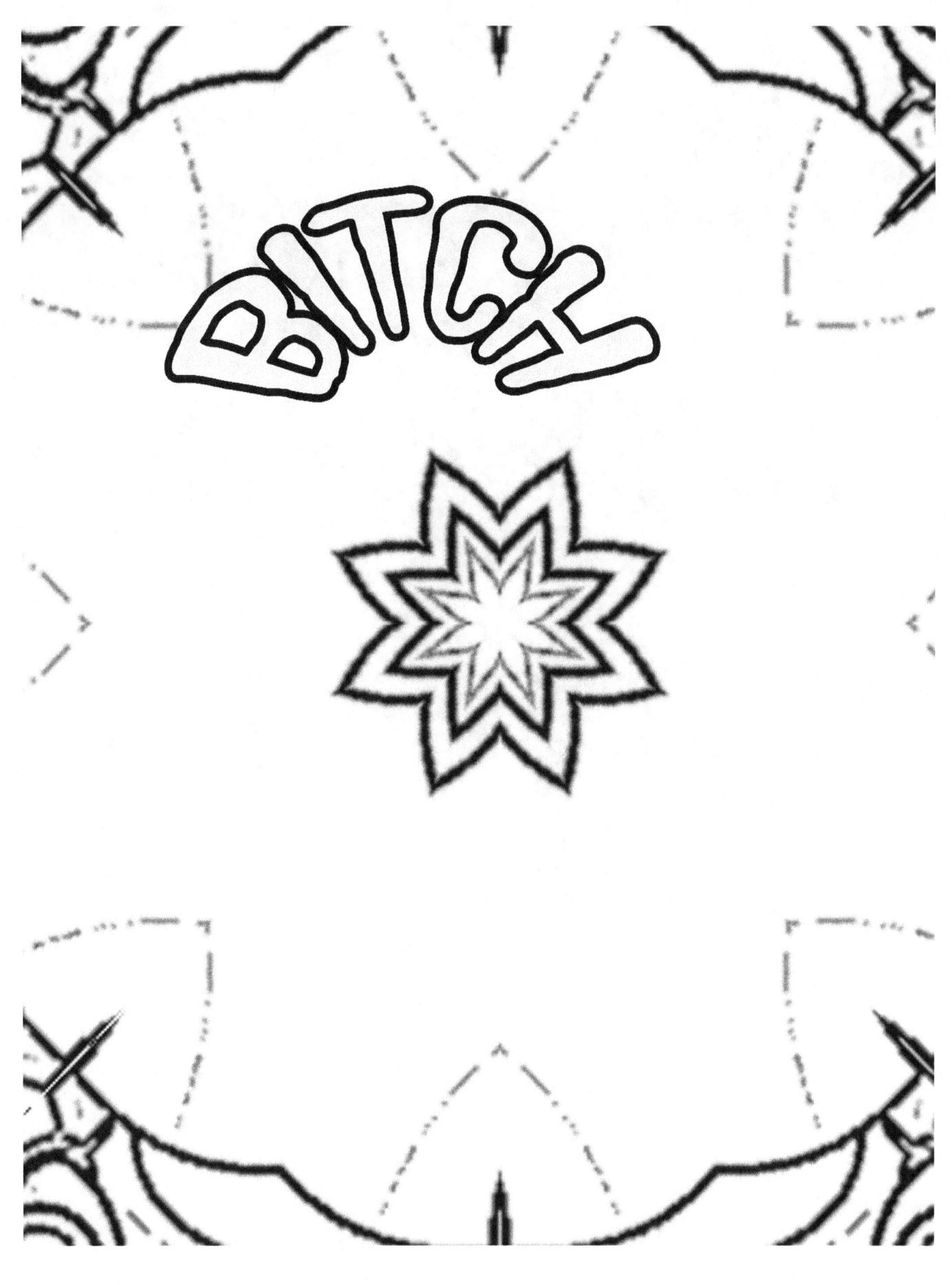

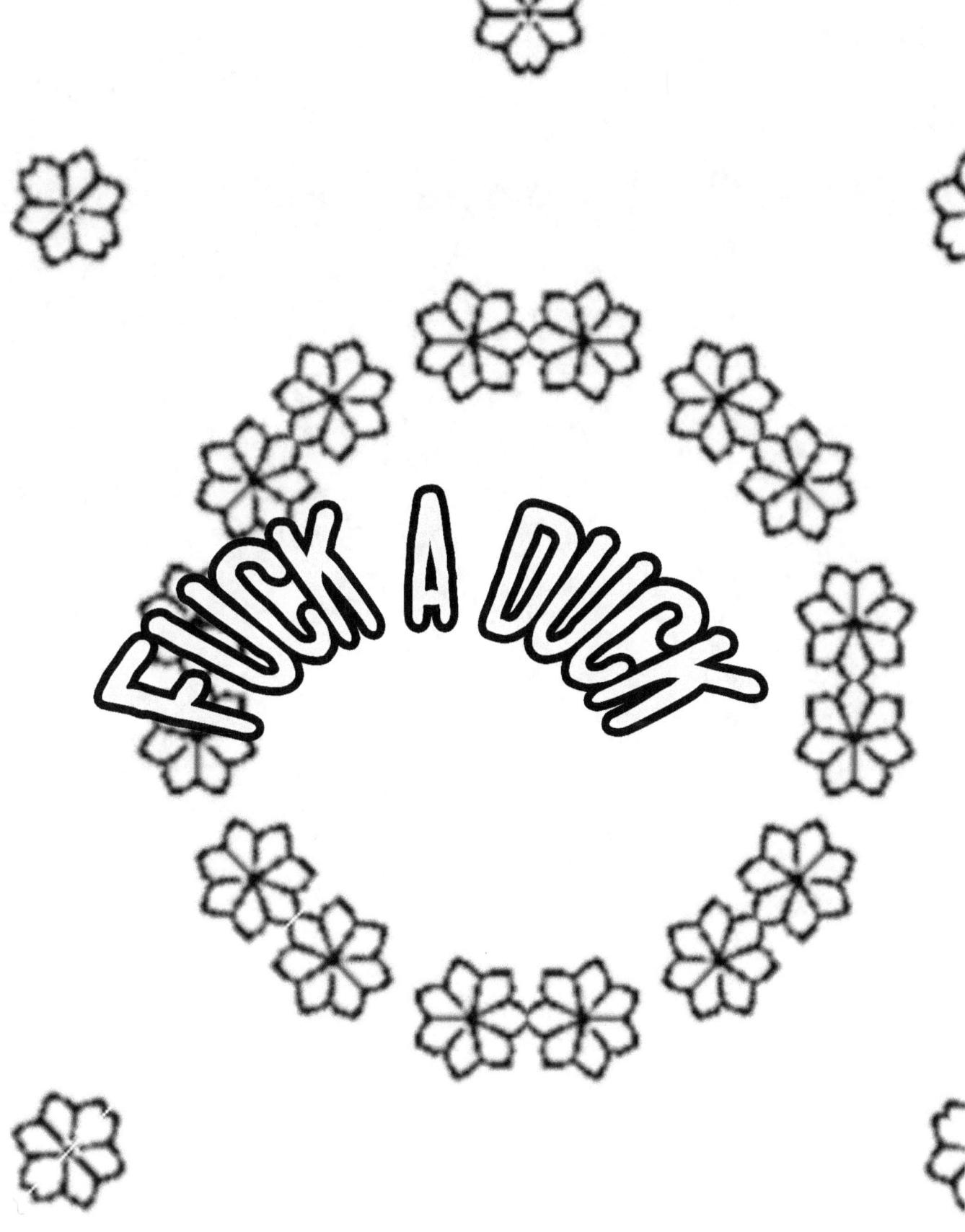

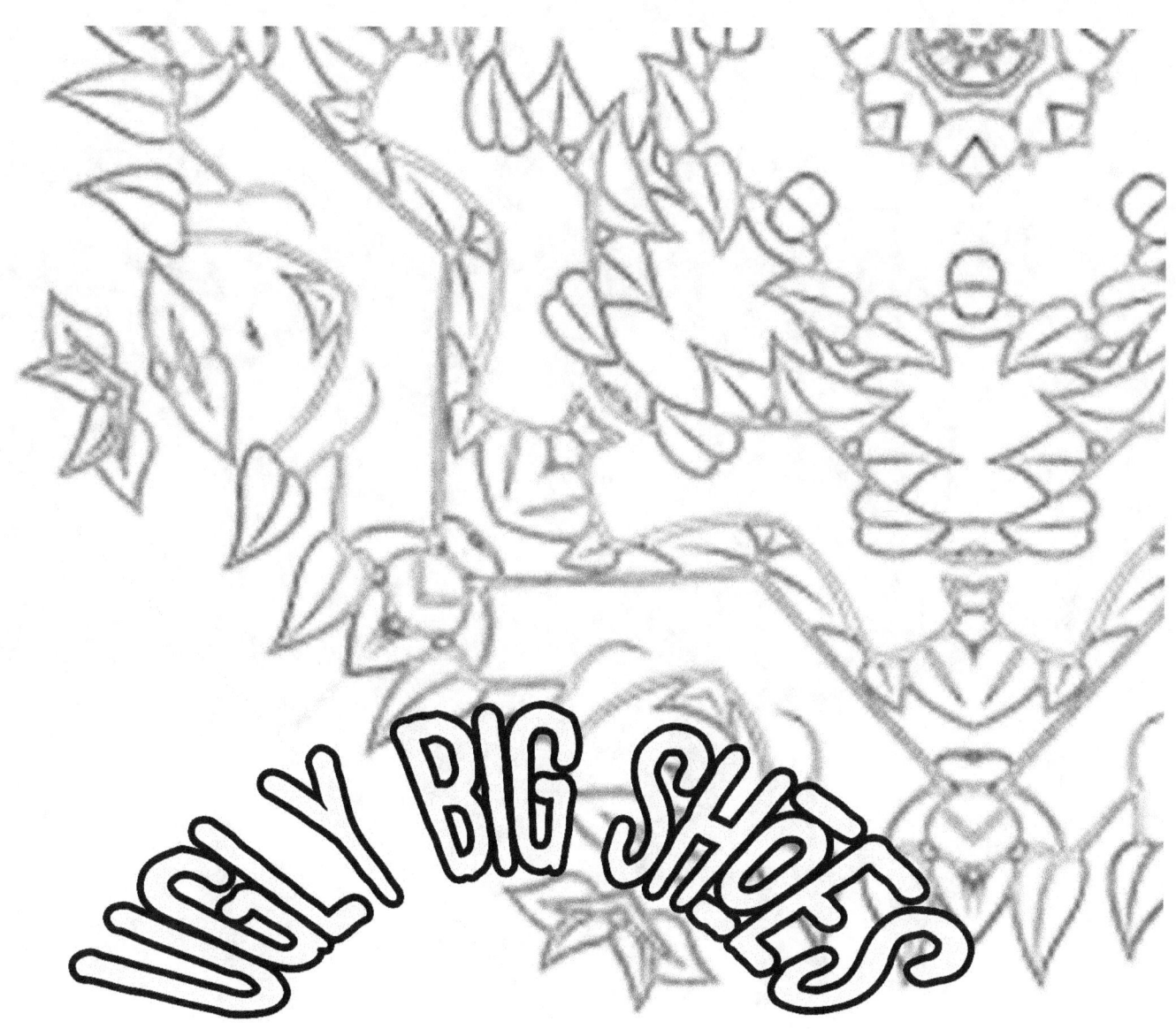

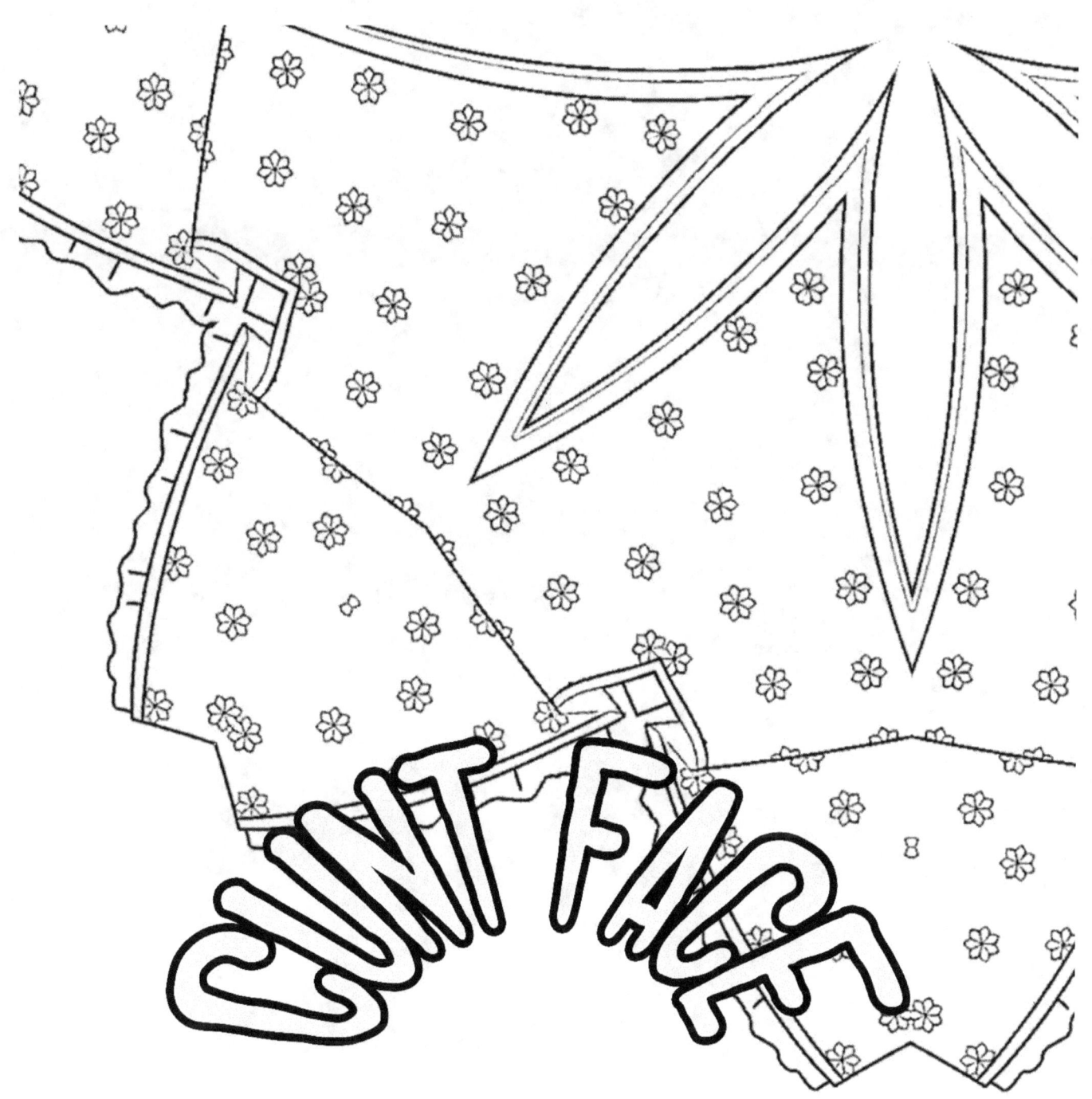

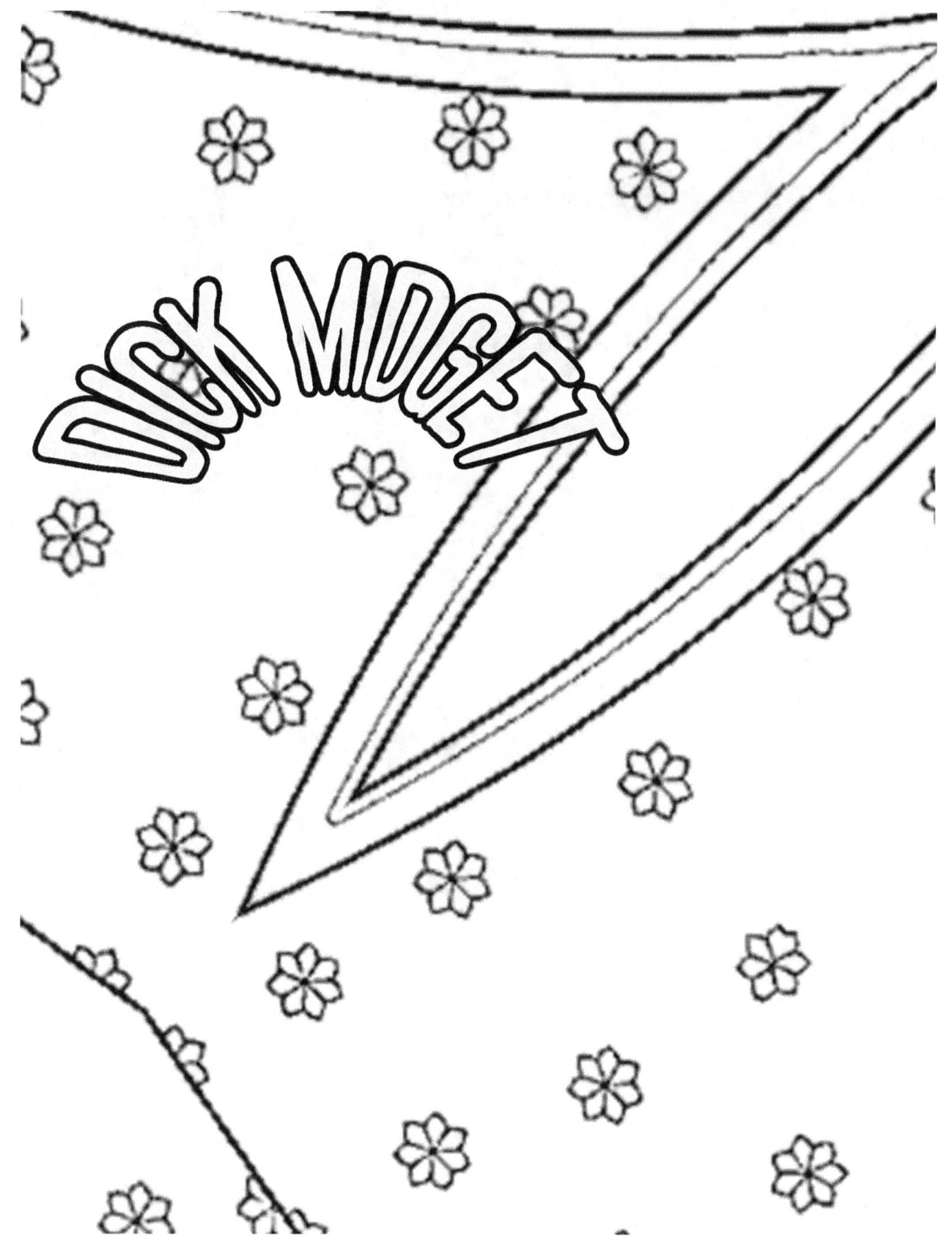

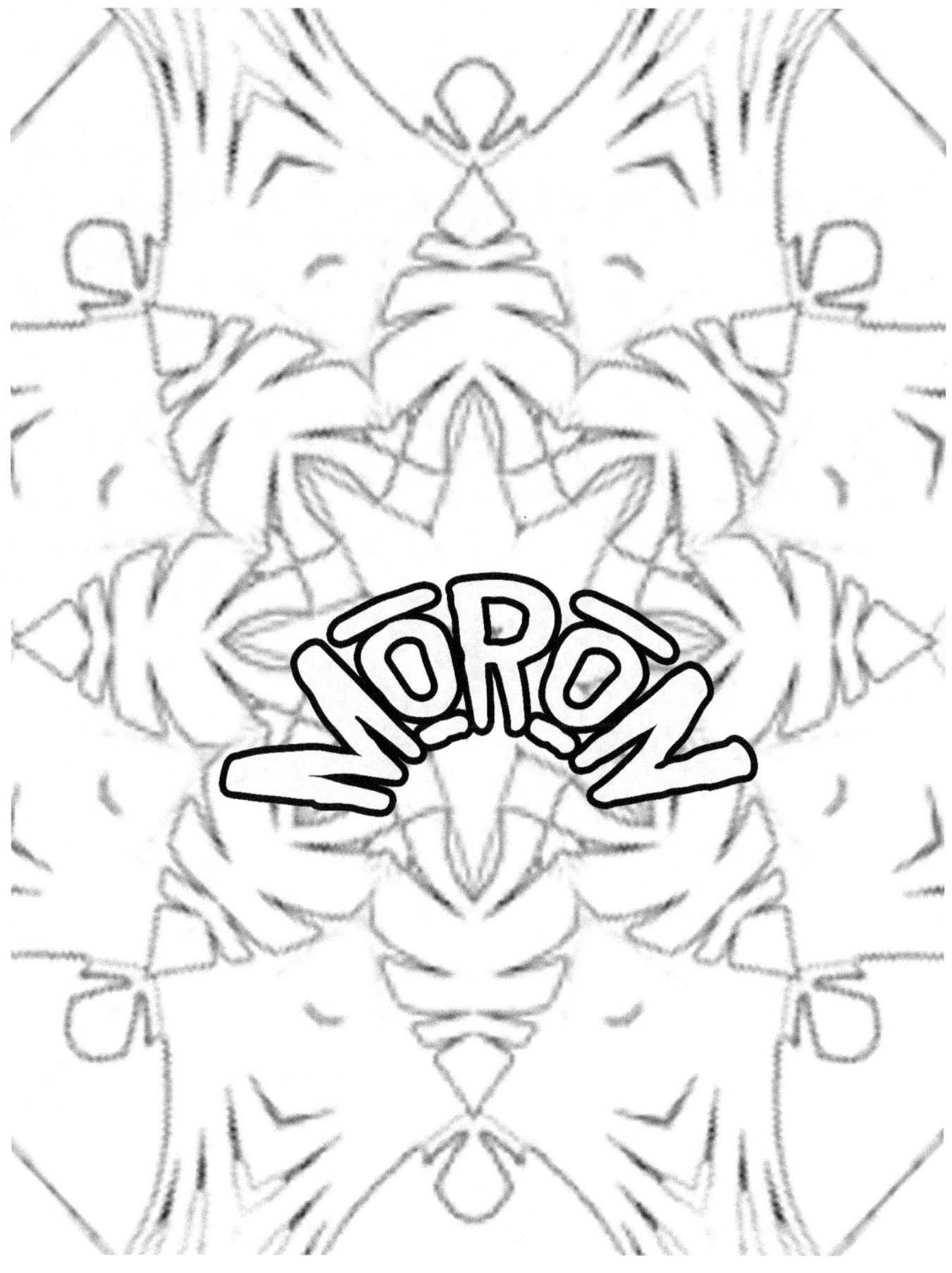

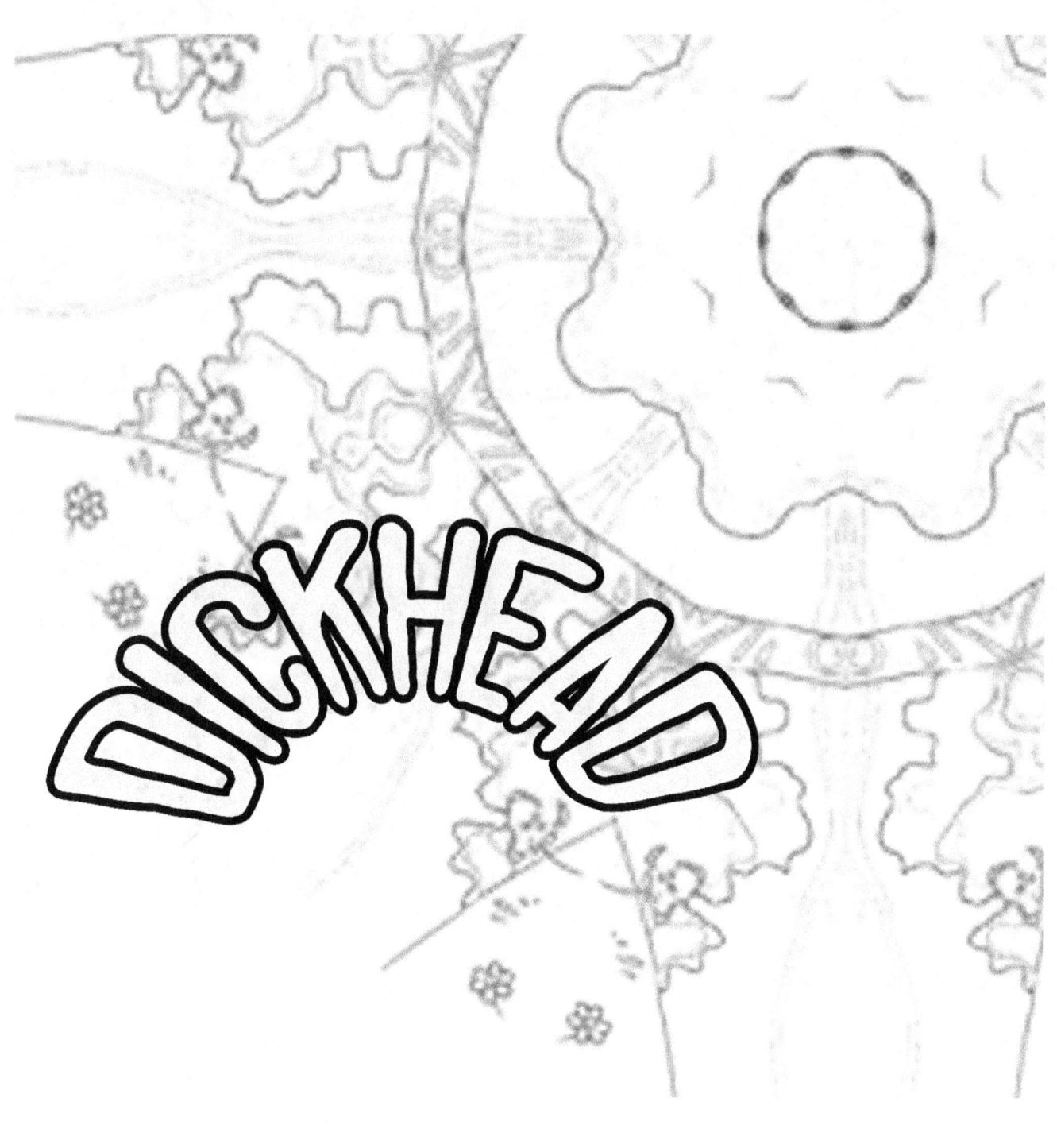

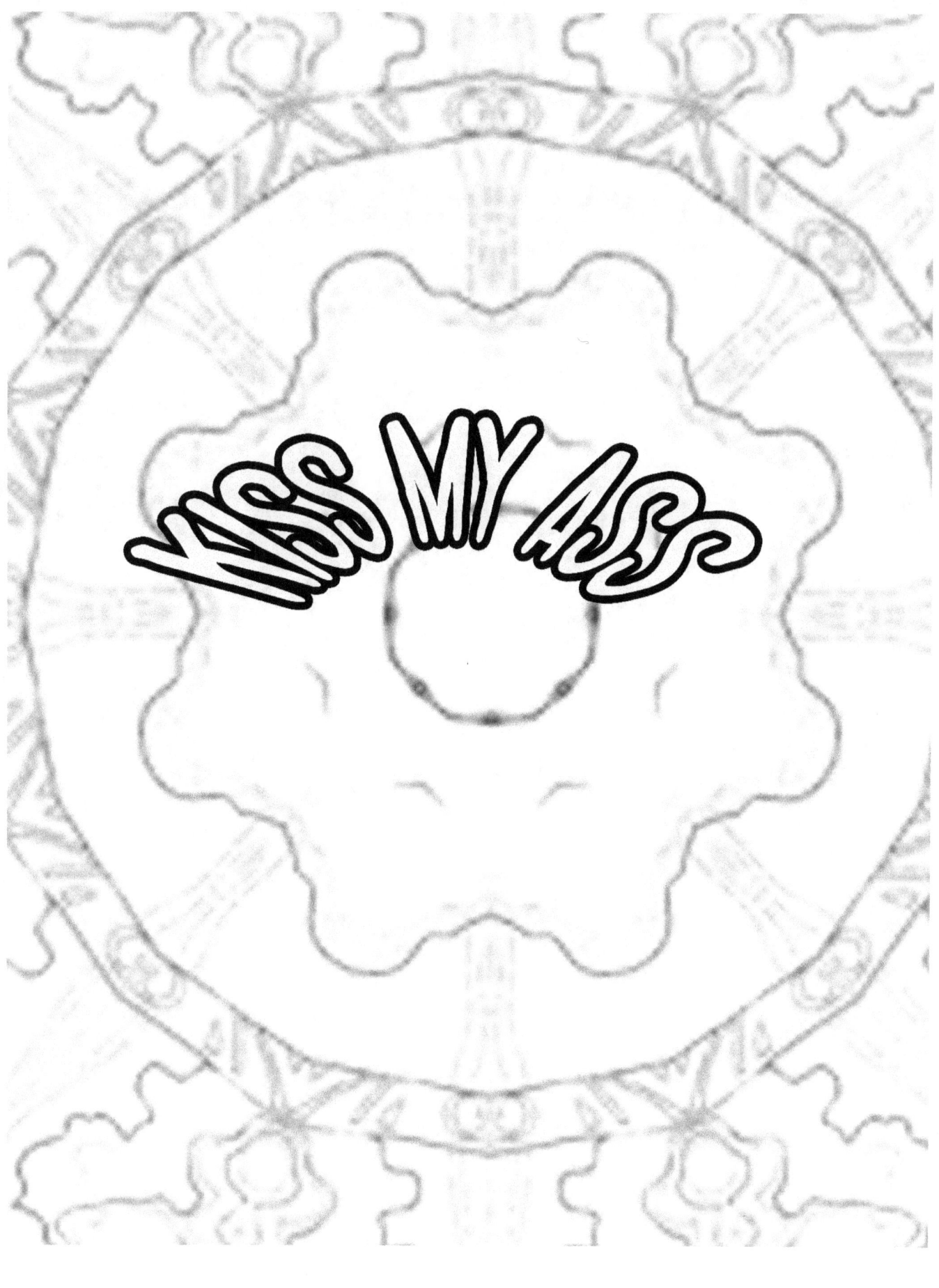

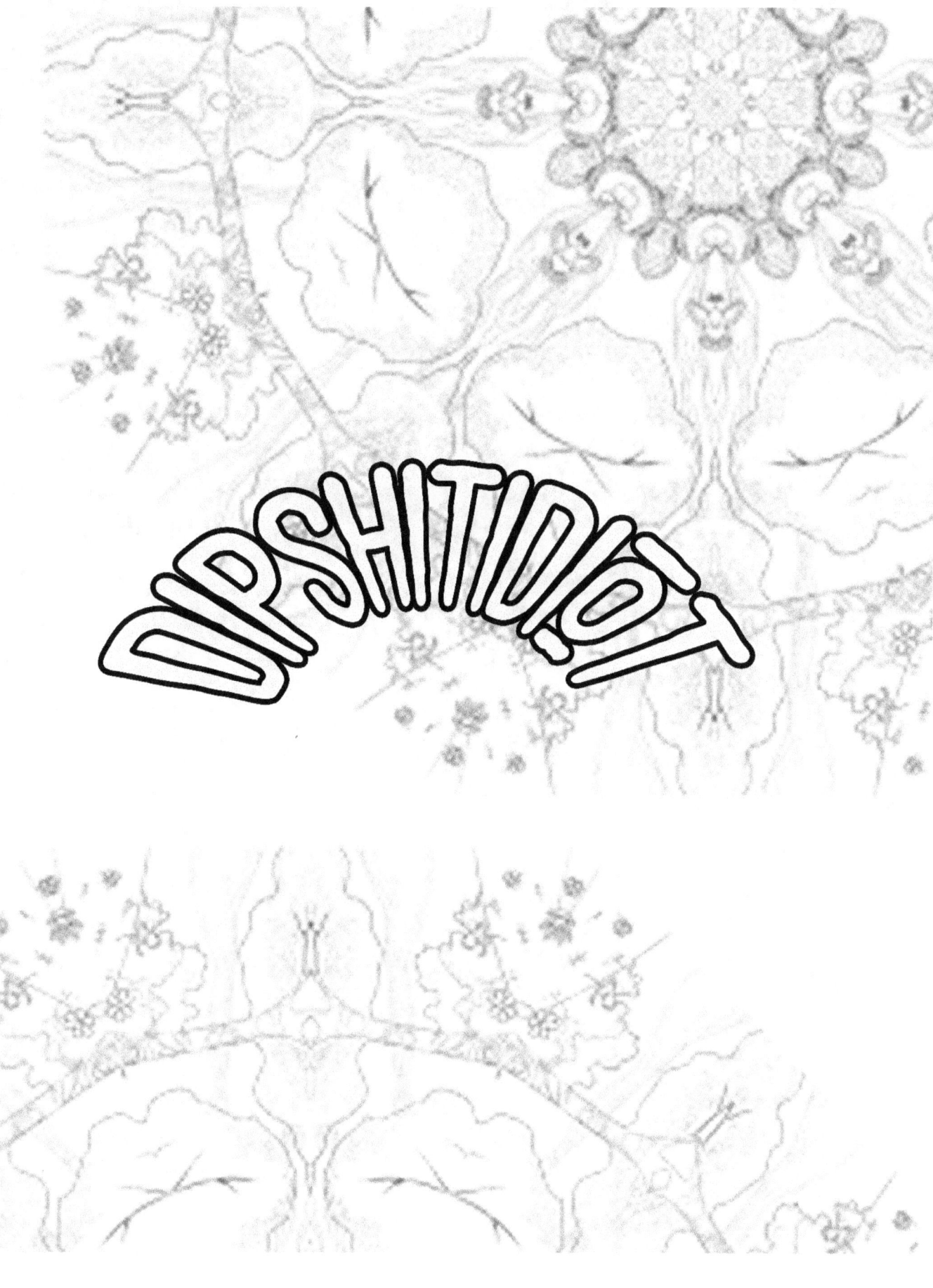

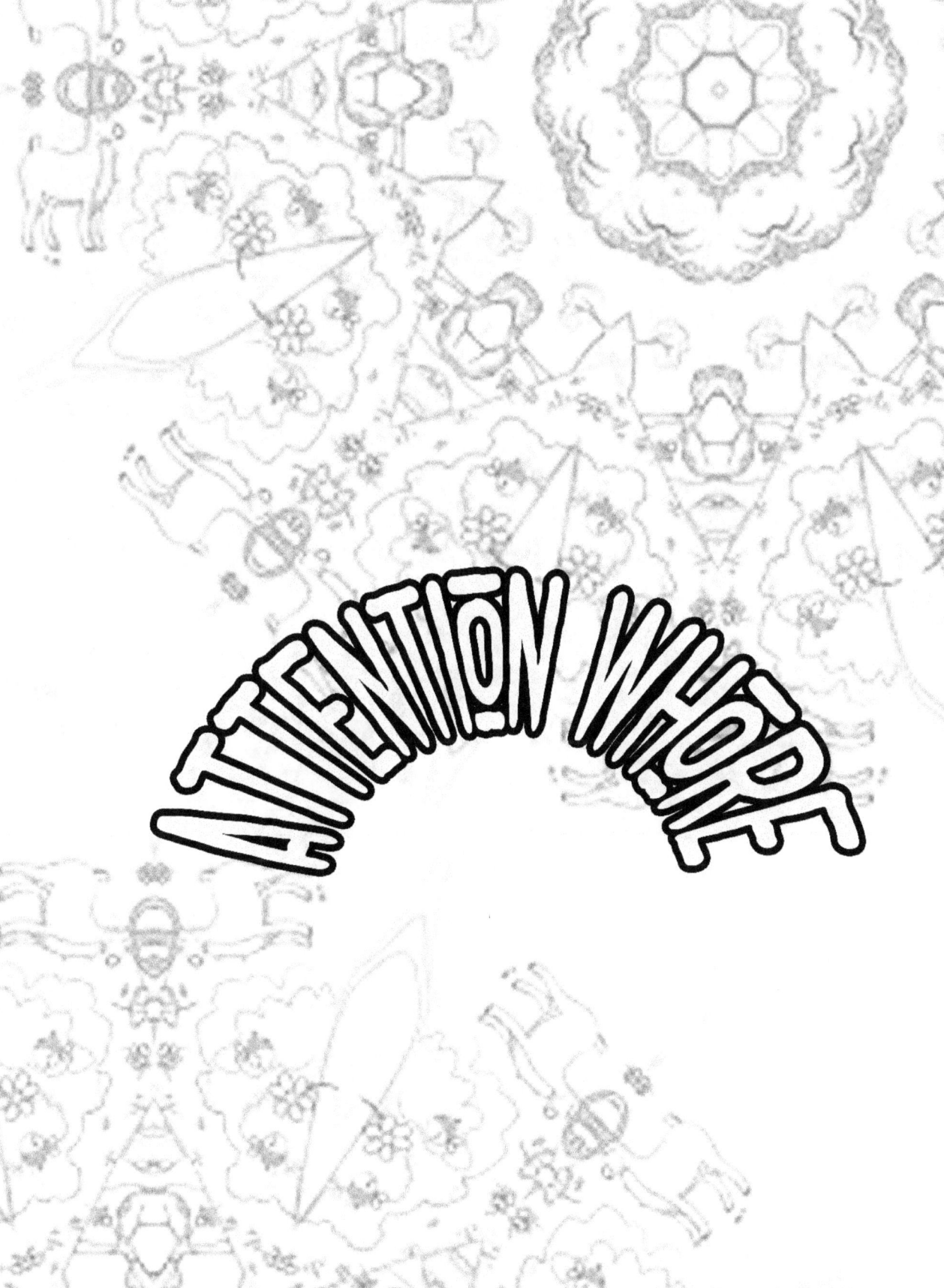

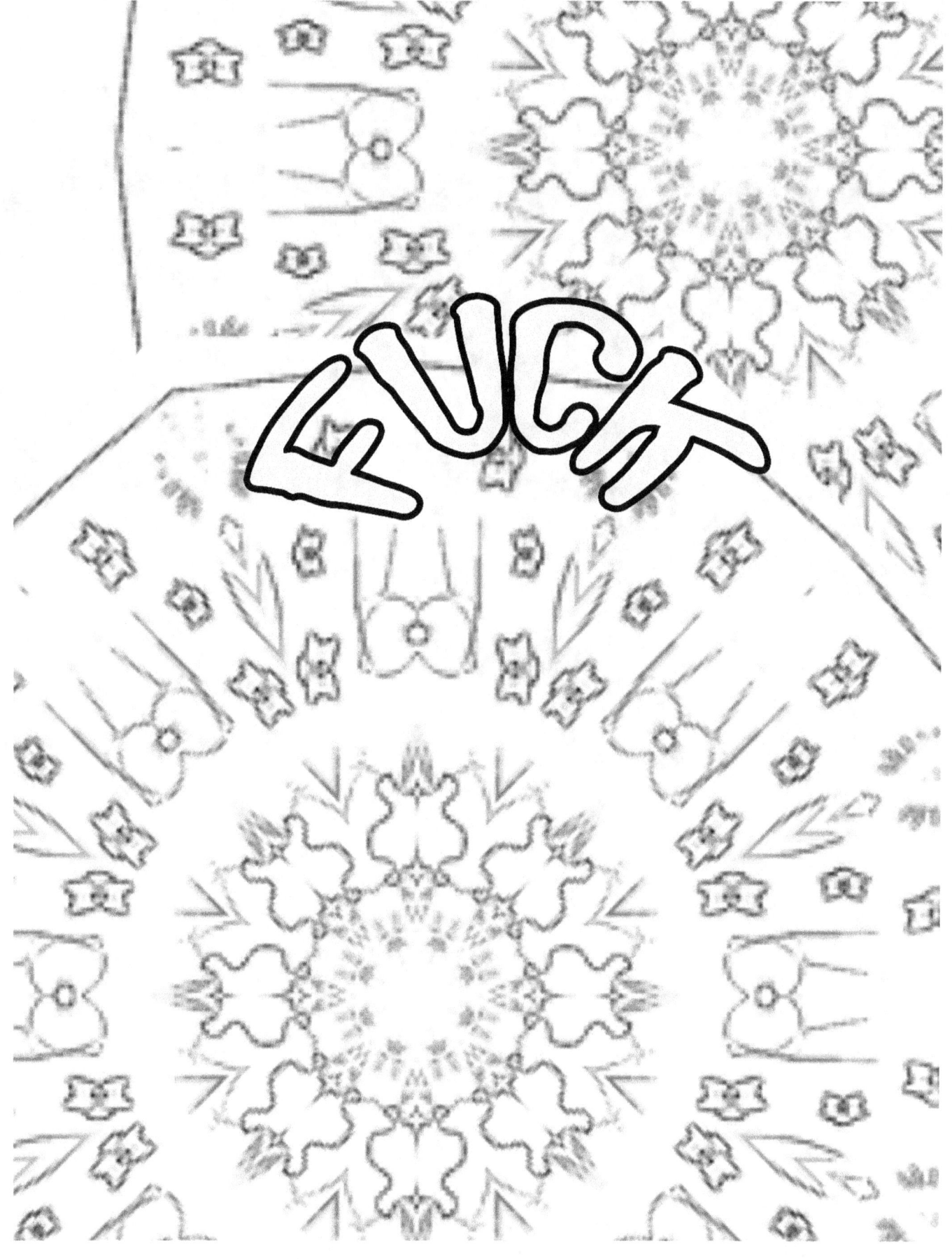

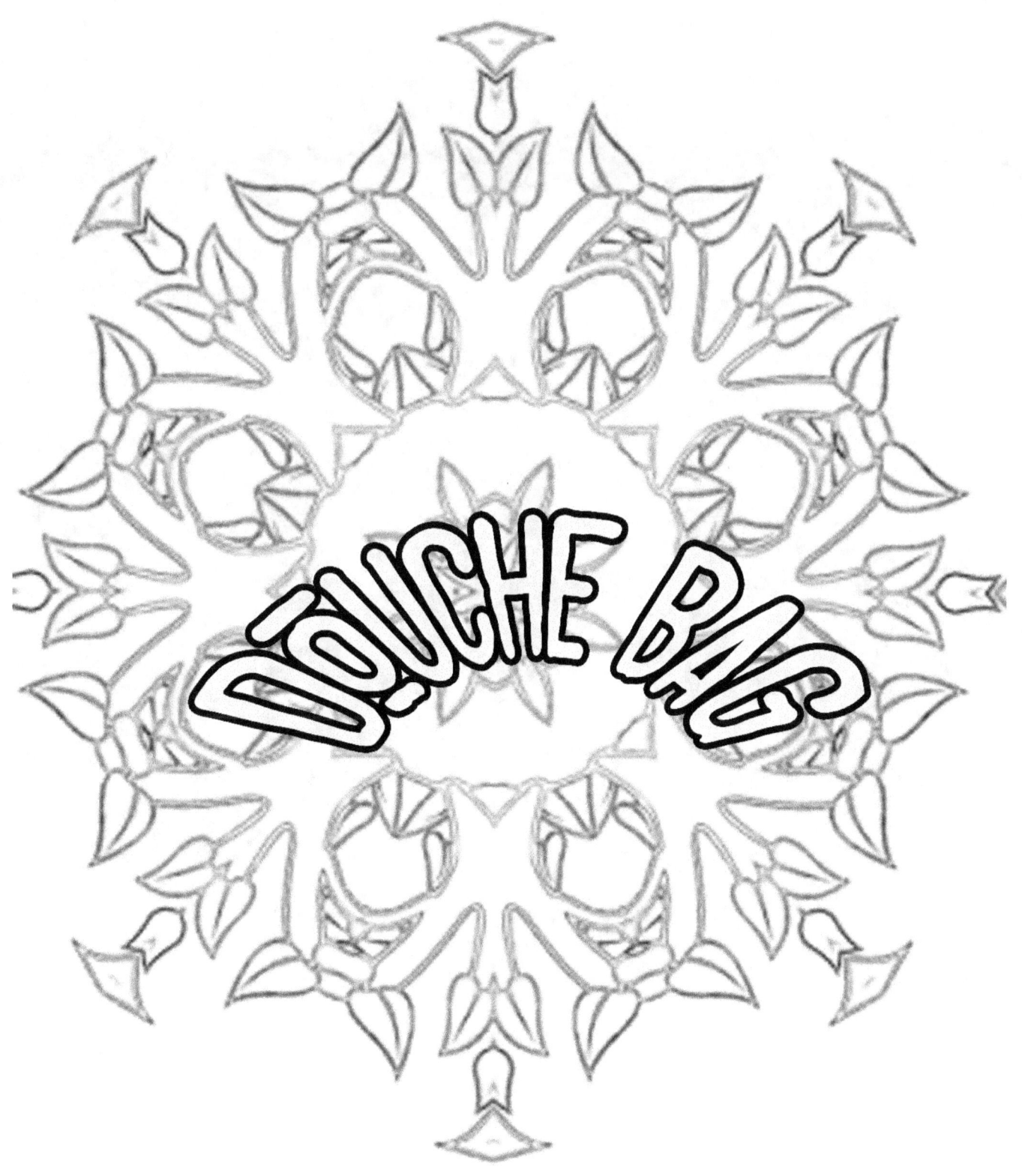

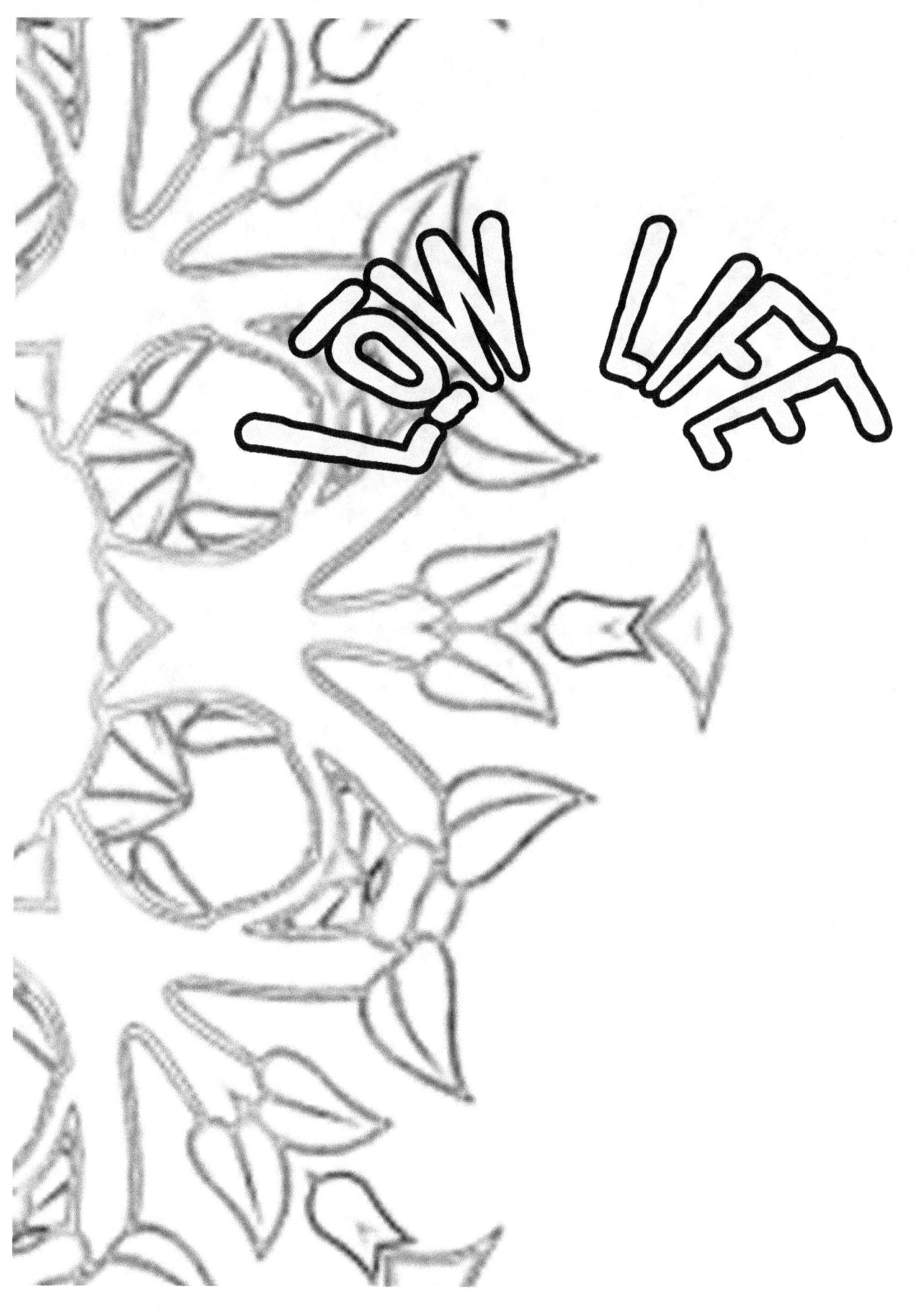

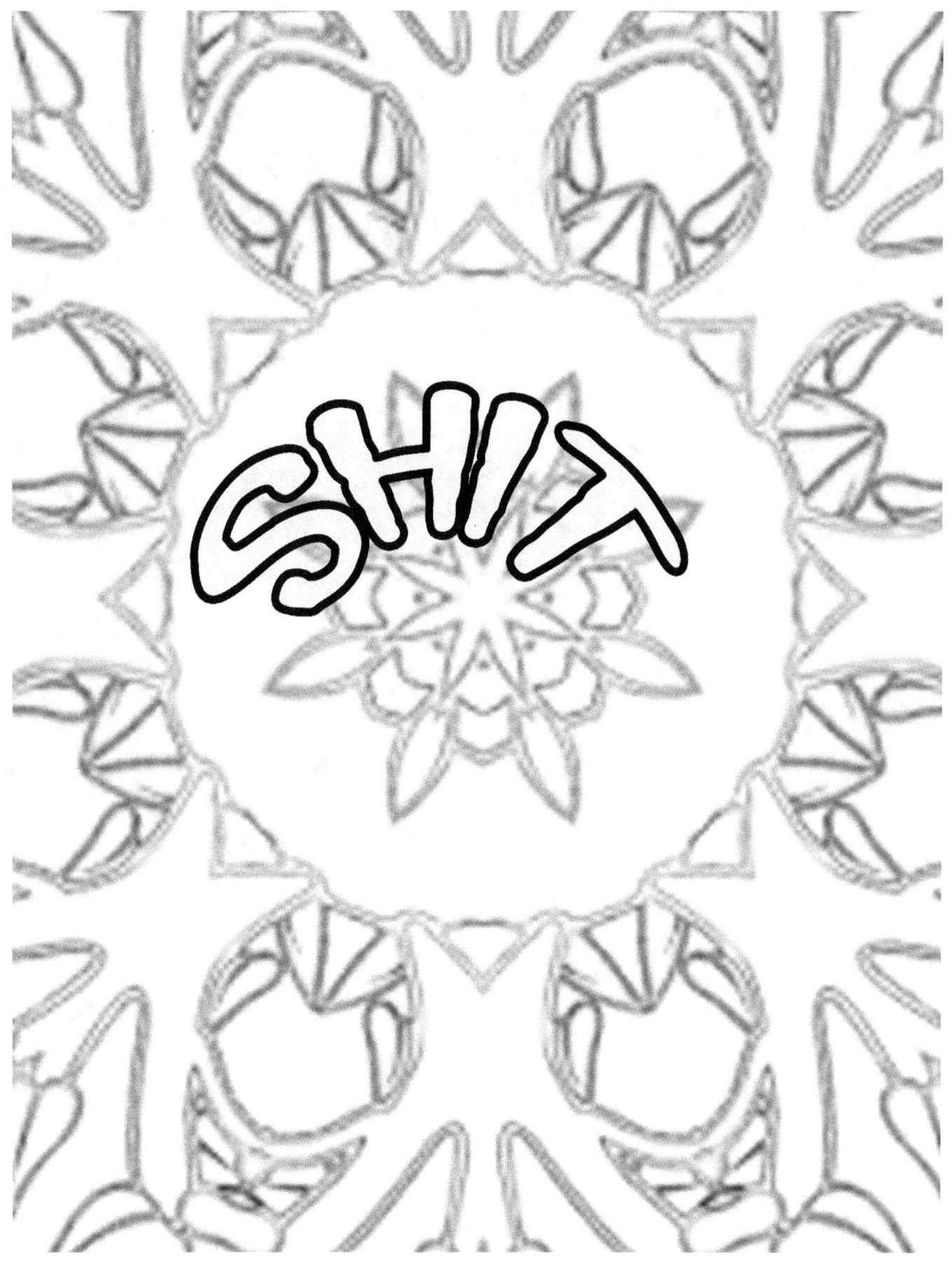

www.ingramcontent.com/pod-product-compliance
Lightning Source LLC
Chambersburg PA
CBHW081748170526
45167CB00009B/3964